A World Where News Travelled Slowly

Lavinia Greenlaw was born in
still lives. She has worked in p
and is now a freelance writer.

LAVINIA GREENLAW

A World Where News
Travelled Slowly

faber and faber
LONDON · BOSTON

First published in 1997
by Faber and Faber Ltd
3 Queen Square London WC1N 3AU

Typeset by Faber and Faber Ltd
Printed and bound in Great Britain by Mackays of Chatham PLC, Kent

A CIP record for this book
is available from the British Library

ISBN 0–571–19160–6

10 9 8 7 6 5 4 3 2 1

for Michael Hofmann

'The telephone wires must be made enormous,
so much goes on along them!'

Derain to Vlaminck, 1901

Acknowledgements

I would like to thank the editors of the following
anthologies and journals in which some of this work was
first published: *Anseo, Columbia, The Guardian, Kris,
London Review of Books, Making for Planet Alice, New
Statesman, New Writing 4, 5 and 6, The New Yorker, The
Observer, The Oxford Magazine, Poetry Review, Poetry
Wales, Times Literary Supplement, Verse.*

'A World Where News Travelled Slowly', 'In a Dark
Room', 'Iron Lung', 'Acquisitions', 'Red Rackham's
Treasure', 'Skin Full' and 'What We Can See of the Sky
Has Fallen' were written during my time as Writer in
Residence at the Science Museum in London. I am grateful
to the Museum for their support.

Some of these poems were first broadcast on BBC
Radio 3.

I would also like to thank the Arts Council of England
for the Writer's Award.

LG

Contents

A World Where News Travelled Slowly

Red Rackham's Treasure

In the last room we found the merman
crouched in a tank of dust,
fiercely articulate but too far gone
for either air or water. A pastiche
of dogs' teeth, cats' claws, paper,
the stale fur of fox or rabbit
and the desiccated tail of a deep-sea fish.

We took the fifty dentists' chairs, the toy
illustrating the evolution of the wheel,
the false weights and measures,
brass plates from surgery doors,
the doctors' walking sticks, the mortsafe
and the charms collected in the field
from the bodies of German soldiers.

Reading Akhmatova in Midwinter

The revelations of ice, exactly:
each leaf carries itself in glass,
each stem is a fuse in a transparent flex,

each blade, for once, truly metallic.
Trees on the hill explode like fireworks
for the minute the sun hits.

Fields hover: bleached sheets in the afternoon,
ghosts as the light goes.
The landscape shivers but holds.

Ice floes cruise the Delaware,
force it under in unnatural silence;
clarification I watch as I watch

the road – nothing but the grind of the plough
as it banks snow, drops salt and grit.
By dark these are just settled hills,

grains embedded in the new fall.
We, too, make little impression
walking back from town at midnight

on birds' feet – ducks' feet on the ramp
where we inch and scrabble our way to the door,
too numb to mind the slapstick.

How did you cross
those unlit, reinvented streets
with your fear of traffic and your broken shoe?

There are mornings when it drips and cracks.
We pull glass bars from railings,
chip at the car's shadow.

Nature

That night at his mother's, the ducks on the pond
– wing-clipped, ornamental, hardly wild –
brought us running from the house.
They were competing to grasp the one
white bird by the throat and force her head
underwater as she skidded in their circle,
climbed the surface, feathers splayed,
hawking up a painful comic cry
I had not understood.

That last visit, out of season,
in the taut thread of our final year.
The air was so weak it could not carry
the smoke from the fire, which did not rise
but found its way by some freak downdraft
to settle in the baby's room.
She neither woke nor altered her breathing
but in the moment it took to reach her,
I stepped through darkness. And did not run

but sat on the wall as the day contracted
to fill the window, confusing the maybugs
caught at the glass and the leaky sill of the door.
Insects I could neither kill nor touch
nor open the latch for, they bumped, collided,
swam towards light. And could not reach it.
Why? Does it have to be like that?

Excursion

We set off from the village to see Attenborough's *Gandhi*
with your usual scoop of the damaged and hopeful:
the priest, the priest's cook, my brother, a manic depressive,
me and a boy I am no longer in love with.
Your adventurous parenting leaves us terrified but free.

Packing us in, you are resentful of seatbelts
and the inadequate neatness of your Vauxhall Chevette
– replacement for some cavernous Estate
with sunk windows and gaping floors.

You bargain with your youngest. He agrees,
nostalgic for the days he was swaddled and tossed
into the back of a Morris Traveller
as, in your dressing-gown, you drove us to school.

Will you jam the lock of the boot or trust it
to stay open to the air
as we lurch forth without a backward thought?

Guidebooks to the Alhambra

Things change, become home and we must leave them.
What do you want? An untouchable sleep
in which I cannot touch you. This heat

opens my skin till I find the strength
to pull at your clothes. Do you remember that palace?
Where the rusted fountain was evidence

of the murder of the Abenceragas cavaliers.
One was found in the hollow trunk of a cypress
with the wife of Aben Hassan – or was it

Muley Abul Hassan, who had his sons decapitated
in the marble hall of the Abencirrajas
to ensure the accession of his second wife's child?

Your distaste for oil and perfume; hours spent washing.
My tongue hesitates on the delicate erosion
of your shoulders and lower back.

Even Irving, who rode through bandit country from Seville
and shared the stairs with the Cockle Queen
and her five husbands, knew it had to be iron oxide.

What We Can See of the Sky Has Fallen

Luke Howard 1772–1864

Born into a lost fortune (the wrong royal attachment
in your *land of reasonable freedom*), a third-generation
Quaker, excluded from the military or church.

A childhood of freak weather – roused from your bed
to see the night lit by a meteor, dim days
of what was later found to have been volcanic smog.

Knowing your expertise and expertly knowing it to be
of the moment – chemistry was *business,* you insisted,
industrial secrets. (What was your role in the manufacture

of ether? The debate whispers on.) You slipped once,
crushing a bottle against your wrist which cut so deep,
the arsenic (*al-zarnik*, orpiment) gilded your veins.

Those weakened hours; the ellipses and questionmarks
of science – *ideas*, you called them, eager to admit
your amateurism, excess Latin baggage and poor maths.

Your ninety-two years held three kings, a queen,
two planets, Faraday and the first photograph.
Somewhere between Income Tax and the Battle of Trafalgar

came your essay on clouds: cool distillations
from your observations' heat. Not giving shape, you found it
and found yourself ever after skybound, abstracted,

frightening the grandchildren with your carnival of apparatus
and unfashionably forceful speech. *People say I am weatherwise,
but I tell them I am very often otherwise.*

Raising thousands for relief of the war-tattered continent,
you disembarked in that half-drowned country
where the language like the rye bread scoured your tongue.

Taking notes on a stork's dance, its nest's construction,
Dutch kindness to cattle, how they walk by their horses,
the Napoleonic roads. The itch of continental quilts,

your infant German, half-grown French, the patchwork
where you took each meal in a different principality,
amused by borders like pub signs stuck in a ditch.

Scrutinising evaporation at a salt works, able to see
banks of snow lift away from a mountain, how the water
of the Rheinfell is nothing if not boiling snow . . .

Goethe's *prodigious inclination to sing the Praises
of Thy Theory of Clouds.* He was avid for the *true observation
of a quiet mind (and such reasonable beliefs!).*

Goethe's request, you first thought a hoax. Reassured
– *one of their very celebrated Poets of Weimar (I think)* –
you sent your life in ten pages. He wrote at least

twelve thousand letters and received eight thousand more.
His effusive note promised a full reply of which there is
no trace in the seven volumes of his life

(something known of every day). You carried a mirror
into the light, insisting you had less to tell than Franklin,
less to pass over than Caesar.

Landscape

A dog's tombstone, its eroded elegy.
Sunk ponds of algae and carp.
A nymph with no arms and improbable breasts.

Dilapidated perspectives
hum with the A-road and InterCity line.

Aroused by emptiness,
you push a hand inside my jeans.

The wind in the three-hundred-year-old
Lebanon cedars
makes a noise like nothing living.

Easter

We got no further than the last available holiday let.
A visitors' book mouldy with good will
towards the owners' 'helpful' children.

An absence of light, a lack of fit;
damp spored behind secondary glazing.
The garden had been politely fenced off.

We trespassed through rhododendrons, rotting magnolia
and bamboo, to glimpse boats moored in the estuary.
Were they only there to be seen?

Further, a cliff shrugged off a baggy line of rusted wire.
We coaxed storage heaters, walked in search of a phone.
For days, the rain hesitated.

The one radio, the one radio station.
Cars edging along the gutted track would be watched coming
for miles.

Last Summer

Not the same road but the same trail of minor incident.
Nothing I see happen, but evidence:
treadmarks, carrion, smashed grass, the odd shoe.

This time I'm alone; not alone, with my daughter,
her fables, her wolf dance, her songs in cod-Arabic.
She twists and pinches a loose tooth.

The engine still has its heady cough, first diagnosed
in a timbered garage on a mini-roundabout
in a county trading on a lost name.

This thing's running on fresh air! Did we laugh?
Do you remember the housemartins that flew semicircles
over the garage eaves, building or feeding?

New Year's Eve

This city's architecture is characterised by the arcades
under which we duck to avoid water bombs. In the square,
a wobbly guitar solo clogged with fuzz leads us to Beppe
whom, ten years earlier, you passed each Sunday
on the cathedral steps, perched on a Harley, just a g-string
in all weathers. Now he is clothed and sells cassettes.

Tonight's celebrations will be broadcast nationwide.
The TV crew erect their twenty-foot friendly animal logo.
In an alley, dancers struggle to dress: three doves, a crow
dark and hooded. We guess the plot and move on.
Midnight finds us eating in a wood-panelled restaurant
where women hang fur coats on hooks by their chairs.

The men, like you, have burnished skin. One tired child
grips a silver evening bag against her silver mohair top.
I have never seen you so drunk, so quizzical or so intent.
You push your tongue against my teeth and issue a warning.
As we leave, a waiter hands me flowers and laughs.
Silent, elated by cold air, we are drawn to each other,

then drawn back, by what sounds like an executioner's drum,
to the square, now paved with broken glass and empty
but for crowd-control barriers and a few impromptu fires.
The police lean dreamily against their cars. We wander off
so you can call your oldest friend. I burn in my sleep.
We send no postcards, take no pictures.

Serpentine

Those buried lidless eyes can see
the infra-red heat of my blood.

I feel the crack, the whisper
as vertebrae ripple and curve.

Days of absolute stillness.
I sleep early and well.

His rare violent hunger,
a passion for the impossible.

He will dislocate his jaw
to hold it.

My fingers trace the realignment
as things fall back into place.

Each season, a sloughed skin
intensifies the colours that fuse

with mineral delicacy at his throat.
Flawless.

Beautiful, simple,
he will come between us.

Last night you found his tooth
on your pillow.

The Shape of Things

There is no eighty-eighth storey
from which to point out three buildings,
each the tallest in its time. I sleep but can't sleep

on the fourth floor of a deluded hotel.
In such an early industrial city,
this is as high, as late as it gets.

I have seen no one, heard only
the sigh of the exoskeletal lift,
the firedoors' groan and cough.

The trill of the Bakelite phone by my bed
I imagine, but not the two ballrooms,
theatrical staircase and slipping lock.

Someone has left a shadow on the carpet
as if, blinded by champagne and erotic waltzes,
they had made a grand unsteady staircase exit

and come to rest with their ear to the ground.
I lie, curl into it, hand on their hand,
neither wanting to be there nor to miss a beat.

The street-cleaning truck scrapes past.
Indecisive, I bring it back
again and again to straighten and empty

my dreams, body heat, talk of political death.
I grasp the receiver when the alarm call comes,
whisper *thank you, thank you* . . .

Invention

for Georgia

My six-year-old mechanic, you are up half the night
inventing a pipe made from jars, a *skiing car*
for flat icy roads and a *timer-catapult*
involving a palm tree, candles and rope.

You could barely stand when I once found you,
having loosened the bars from the cot
and stepped out so simply you shocked yourself.
Today I am tearful, infatuated with bad ideas,

the same song, over and over. You take charge,
up-end chairs, pull cushions under the table,
lay in chewing-gum and juice,
rip newspaper into snow on the roof.

Back through the Window

The torn-off shout
of a boy swerving past
on his bike

points toward nightfall
if not darkness.
Since morning

the rhythm and bounce
of building work
has passed back to back

among these tall houses.
It will end unnoticed,
its acoustic borrowed

by a loop of bells
from a church I've not seen
open or entered.

Drivers caught
in these unpassable streets
drop gear to negotiate.

No argument
in the eager yelp
of remote-locking systems:

each car's obedient jump
ticks by unnoticed,
unlike the blurt

of a wayward alarm.
Ice-cream sellers?
Ambulance crew?

The singing insomniac
walks over the hill
in the briefly peculiar light at 3.30.

Skin Full

I laugh till my jaw unhinges,
we hold me in with ribboning fingers.
Moderation in moderation. Who said that?
It makes extraordinary sense to me.

You say that life is a three-legged race.
They show us the door and we have some difficulty,
bound like that from thigh to ankle.
The street is a blanket. We will sleep

with you on your front, me on your back.
The night will be endless and we will be endless,
layer on layer, infinitely warm.
I sing as we lie shoulder to shoulder

and tell you there is no such thing as anything
that is not a small circle. Now it is morning.
Can the bones we broke out of be mended?
My eyes . . . The sun picks over their embers.

Hayseed

The city is baked and blown by incontinent, sudden weather.
The trees are luminous or racing. It changes,
it is not something we can predict.
The catch of pollen, ozone, exhaust in my throat

is unbreathable, secret, and for this same reason
my tears are yellow and viscous, and cannot cool
the shot capillaries of my eyes. You are waiting to fly.
Even the airport has its airport gods. I pray

they urge you return to your lover. A princess,
it has been said, but one somewhat lacking in courage.
Whatever. My teeth in your shoulder, my salt on your fingers,
a hayseed in your heel.

Calibration

In these dazed weeks of absence and immediacy,
the nights rarely drop below seventy.
The hill has its nightlife, amiable, averted.

Some bring candles, blankets and books,
others fall down. This privacy is teenage,
collective, no one is fooled or cares;

not the park police, who swivel the beam
from the roof of their patrol truck to catch
what is only, after all, someone running without intent.

We swarm, tucked under the roof, compelled
by the tinsheet-flashlight dramatics of a storm
at three a.m. I am furious with joy

at catching you, for the first time, in momentary sleep.
The mosquito bites strung out along my right side
from thigh to ankle, will erupt and itch.

Tryst

Night slips, trailing behind it
a suddenly innocent darkness.
Am I safe, now, to slip home?

My fists tighten your collar, your fingers
lock in my hair and we hover
between discretion and advertised purpose.

Dawn traffic in both directions,
taxis, milk floats, builders' vans.
Each proposes a service or poses a threat

like the police, slumped couples in cars
left to patrol each other, to converge
at a red light that stops little else.

Each separation is outweighed
by more faith, more sadness;
accumulated static, the shock in every step.

I go to sleep where my life is sleeping
and wake late to a fused morning,
a blistered mouth.

Naevi

The cautery's sear: these beads of blood
that have taken all winter, all spring,
to collect minutely, evaporate in seconds.
No promises! The doctor's benevolent uncertainty.

Cadastre

Our two houses have decreed a show of worth,
to be historical, financial and public.

Onto the streets come the investments,
the deeds, shares, equity and interest,

the clean linen, empty closets
and children – deployed first with the silver,

then with the guns. Family arms
are flexed, safety catches lifted,

credit cancelled, pictures painted,
goalposts shifted, spit and polish

left to dry. The people come
to settle provenance and provocation

(there is always someone shouting).
In the final count the adulterers

are overlooked. They are less than salt
– a once-prized commodity

for which our two houses have little use
other than to add taste, loose stains, open the road.

What's Going On

The demolition crew are petulant.
Swinging the ball, they could lay bets and lose.
We cannot help but stand in the street,
smile up at the light where half the roof
has fallen away and the sky comes at us
from all three sides through a couple of windows,
surprisingly large and somehow intact.

In a Dark Room

Not long after it was thought reasonable
to lower the blinds on windows
when passing through the Alps,

Fox Talbot's sketches of Lake Como
from the camera obscura were pitiful.

*

Watching a bottle of salts go dark.
Chancing upon the correct, imperfect solution.

Lace, leaves, anything complicated and flat.
Laura was delighted, called them 'shadows',
wrote for more as they faded.

No Particular Horse

Horses would fashion their gods as horses.
                                    Xenophanes

Horses with wings and horses with shoes.
White stallions sacrificed to Roman gods.
Scythian kings buried with fifty horses.

Horse sense: a perpetual expectation
of danger. Cave dwellers drove herds
over cliffs for an easy killing.

*

Drawings found in a tomb suggest
the Ancient Egyptians were among the first
to ride horses.

Warm bloods, stud books,
a government incentive for the Irish Draught,
the only ever accidental Cob,

the Arab's dished face and seventeen ribs,
the recessive Albino, chosen mount
of the Lone Ranger and Emperor Hirohito.

*

Horse points, fetlock and foreleg.
As in football or driving,
an offside.

Gervase Markham's horse skeleton
('worse than approximate') misled readers
for twenty-one editions and a hundred years

until Auzoux's papier-mâché model,
each flayed muscle, artery and bone
labelled with scraps of Latin and French.

*

The horse in war, legendary siege-breaker
turned fast offensive transport.
Army vets botching it with gas masks,

paraffin salve and cocaine. Running my hand
along the hooked spine of a broken-backed
roan crippled by a bite from his father.

*

How we still measure distance from on horseback.
Matisse driven at a walking pace
to keep *a sense of the trees*.

Fox Talbot on a train in 1838,
wanting to go no faster than that.
My childhood horse future

of great escapes, crossing the desert
on a wall-eyed skewbald, leaving it
up to the horse gods. Horse talk.

I can offer no greater sign of trust
than to say you are someone with whom
I would steal horses.

Acquisitions

Henry Ford boasted
there would be no Egyptian mummies in his museum.

Everything we have is strictly American.
Steam engines, cars and guns

in answer to the amateur anthropologist's
list of set questions:

Is bleeding, scarifying or cupping practised?
Is marriage by capture, exchange or purchase?

The Oasis in Winter

This is rare.
Three inches of snow on the dunes
and the golf course sunk.

Walk the five-mile beach
without interruption, no shingle or curve.
Strangers:

watch them rise
to the surface of your vision and fall
from the corner of your eye.

The rocks at the end
are the rocks you would have believed as a child
to be legendary.

What happens?
The gothic shriek of a sea bird.
You crunch and slip, bewildered by tenses:

dying fish, spent fuel, fresh air
and here, a pool of caught salt water.
If you must speak, speak quietly.

Islands

This passion for iron,
their *metal from heaven*,
the heaviest element
created by fusion
at the heart of a star
which then collapses,
folding and folding
till the core explodes
to scatter and settle
within the triangle
of past, present, future
– all possible worlds.

Millefiori

to Don Paterson

He preferred his glass eye to be of itself,
vitreous not ocular
or even optically convincing.

Without pupil or iris, allowed to risk
its stubbornly fluid nature,
the blue held everything.

It liquefied candlelight
and clouded over in winter.
Once, at the opera, an aria

built wave upon wave of sound,
higher and closer till it struck
the resonant frequency

of blue glass
and the molecules of his eye
oscillated into a thousand flowers.

Iron Lung

The ventriloquist's breath;
watch, while my lungs compress
it is the concertina pump that sighs.

Not a glass coffin, more obscure,
a dark room I cannot go into
but am locked into from the neck.

The pressure:
your hand on the small of my back,
a whispered imperative, I rise and fall.

The recovery of tension, I dream of it –
through a window, adjacent trains in a station,
how one must be moving if the other is still.

Snow Line

It was wet & white & swift and where I am
we don't know. It was dark and then
it isn't.

John Berryman

Dying wasps crawl into shoes, settle and curl.
I find them, wings askew, staggering up window-panes.
They have lost an element to play in and must
rebalance their weight. The call I want to make

is ill-timed, unanswerable. A dream I had or wanted?
There is snow, feet deep on the overheated hill
and falling. I walk slowly, lie down in it with care.
All that talk when it could be simple!

A Changeable Province

Each district has its palace, monumental
steps, an empire of local causes,

red tape. The Roman ruins are cordoned off
so a young archaeologist can dust

a frieze of weapons, profiles and fruit.
The city has buried its treasure, consigned

its best works to a back room and a guard
who bulges out of the gloom like a rhizome,

rooted to the spot. Only a tourist's flashbulb
can force him into some kind of life.

The famous terraces have been propped up
by privet and a dozen replica sphinxes.

In the historic quarter, lanes tilt at angles
that make their prosperous frontages look

a little less smug. Sex toys, cigarettes
and chocolate are sold the old-fashioned way,

through sex. Election posters are neutral,
all eyes and teeth. A Ferris wheel disappears

into the night. Its shadowy spokes
assimilate easily but the dates, initials,

arrows and hearts that cover the worn wood
of its cabins keep some kind of score.

Mainland

Why is it I can get no further than the weather,
a flat sky pressing clouds to the earth, clouds simmering
on mountains, glacial volcanoes boiling up a flood?

No fire in the cool late sun we slide away from.
What else is there to do after months offshore
but march into town in seaboots and ceremonial dress?

A World Where News Travelled Slowly

It could take from Monday to Thursday
and three horses. The ink was unstable,
the characters cramped, the paper tore where it creased.
Stained with the leather and sweat of its journey,
the envelope absorbed each climatic shift,
as well as the salt and grease of the rider
who handed it over with a four-day chance
that by now things were different and while the head
had to listen, the heart could wait.

Semaphore was invented at a time of revolution;
the judgement of swing in a vertical arm.
News travelled letter by letter, along a chain of towers,
each built within telescopic distance of the next.
The clattering mechanics of the six-shutter telegraph
still took three men with all their variables
added to those of light and weather,
to read, record and pass the message on.

Now words are faster, smaller, harder
  . . . *we're almost talking in one another's arms.*
Coded and squeezed, what chance has my voice
to reach your voice unaltered and to leave no trace?
Nets tighten across the sky and the sea bed.
When London made contact with New York,
there were such fireworks, City Hall caught light.
It could have burned to the ground.

Underworld

What if you have swallowed me,
swallowed six pomegranate seeds
and split your life? Must I let you go
down alone into each night as winter,
the path behind you freezing over?

Will I learn not to cry after,
to lie still on the ice, to know this is
not for ever, that the sky will crack
and I will fall through and wake with you
in something of summer?

Our Life as Friends

This is the world in which we did not
get married. The paper and gold
to prove otherwise are stuck in the realm
of potential, like Aristotle's chair in its tree.
The day is its own machine. It passes
the time. At odd, pivotal moments
we are pulled past each other,
dumb, smiling, locomotive,
carried away . . . our families yawn
and swallow us up with all the love
of sad but hungry giants. At night,
we concentrate. Our houses adjust,
billow and tilt by less than inches.
A trip switch ignites the boiler,
keeps old water at an even simmer,
the fridge cranks up when it needs
to cool down. Your guilt is asleep.
You have not opened my eyes.
What grows? The lopped ash
fills my window when it's able.
After each cutback, its roots subside.
Each scene of our lives is familiar,
the details simplified, as if an unstable
picture varnish were clouding the view.
There is no atmosphere. Nothing lingers
in the air. Tall stories, bad ideas,
bounce off satellites back down to earth.
This is the world that will not be shaken.
The sky is a dome and we are not
beyond it, slipping, heads still turning,
our fingerprints all over the glass.

Trees in Nine Windows

They have us surrounded, drowned out by machinery:
the rasp and saw of cicadas, digital percussive frogs.

Birdsong is the languid creak of a stiff bicycle,
punctuated by a woodpecker's pneumatic bursts.

From somewhere beyond the leaves comes the bleat of a drill.
Our radiators hiss as they digest the first heat of their season.

Scoraig; Maine

This could be your part of Scotland but the panther,
no hoax, grows fat on snowshoe hare.
Cars are forced off the road, not by leering sheep
but moose, rickety beasts, they hang their heads.

Unsupplanted (no tax breaks), trees find safety
in numbers. They grow into the wind, grow so old
the creep of a maple leaf blown across the tarmac,
caught in headlights, casts a human shadow.

You live on a peninsula but a mountain forces you
to start each journey at sea, to arrive
at your wedding by trawler, to ferry tractor parts
on the wheezy strength of an outboard motor,

to wheelbarrow everything over the hill.
Here, each island is locked in place
by a bridge or causeway so well made
that the limping suspension of this old Ford Mercury

sleeps through to Stonington. On the edge of town,
our name is on the gate of a site for mobile homes
(a family trade in vacancies?) and again,
emblazoned on a fuel truck as it takes a blind corner

on the wrong side, where I am now walking
down to the shoreline which cannot be reached
without trespass (our childhood spent in other people's
boats and trees). Your coastal post round,

EU paperwork, subsidised growth of tiny oak
and ash and beech. Three lives make a living.
I pass our name a final time, loosely pegged
to the last mailbox inside the town line.

Five O'Clock Opera

This cavernous apartment is ours on four months' good will,
like the industrial washing-machine and pocket transistor:
our two kinds of noise. What else? My mother's letters
to my daughter; a subscription to delayed world news;
and a campaign of love-hate mail, broken-hearted
socialist realism, agony and baby talk.

The local radio station is on a sponsorship drive.
They raise the stakes each hour, as desolate and righteous
as their featured diva who is climbing ever higher
in the mountains, her echo fitfully insistent
on the last word. The clocks have already gone back.
Our afternoon gets caught in the dark.

Minus Ten

The snow is blameless. It falls like someone
who cannot stop talking, in querulous drifts.
It covers the same ground we barely remember,
collects evidence wherever we slip.

Thaw turns to ice, freezing the surface
to a single assertion. We must break glass
with every step to reach a starting point.
And the children. What of the children?

Tenure

The rat man, with his company shirt
and brochure of vermin, calls this house
old and *fine*. It is middle-aged, ill fit
and given to hoarding the weather.
The walls are porous and, now, baited.

At night, something in the crawlspace whimpers.
We deafen each other, we bury our heads;
whatever shapes are made, however we shift
in sleep, someone keeps hold. This is not home
but we wake in its borrowed silence, possessed.

The pile of logs unearthed for a fire
falls softly to pieces, all used up
by the natural claims of insects and birds.
Lichen and spores make poor insulation:
this wood sifts heat and is stupidly easy to burn.

The Coast Road

The avenues peter out in the two hundreds.
From there it's small fields, small businesses
secluded at the end of swept drives:
rare breeds, topless bars, revivalist churches,
sunset homes. Something for everyone,

lost or found. For whatever reason
your grief stalls long enough for you to want
something for us of this day. The road
gets straighter and somehow older.
The swamp is dense but sticks to the edge

of each broad, clipped verge. We stop
so you can show me cat fish, cypress knees,
Spanish moss, all petrified shades of smoke,
ash, straw, cinder. How can I tell
what's growing from what's already dead?

A rosy glint is an armadillo. Preoccupied,
quivering, it flicks its tail and forages off,
road-blind, nose in the air. I am delighted,
so you find them for me again and again,
and I tell you what I've heard, that armadillos

are not indigenous to Florida but came north
with a circus, met a hurricane, broke loose
and here they are, pink and gold and thriving
up to a point. Then the trees give way to sky,
the air carries more salt than mud.

Egrets wobble into view, so white
and lacking in detail with their stretched necks
and linear heads, they seem to be missing.
The fish houses are roped off, gutted, safe
only for pelicans, stale birds down on their luck.

We trace power lines out to the islands.
The industrial chimney stacks could be Mexico.
There's a mile or so of the open shoreline
we hoped for and we make it last,
each small step on oyster shells.

p.p.

You are not there to hold my head.
I have it in my hands.

Amanuensis,
I take note, guard your secrets.

It pleases me – impersonator –
to witness my forgery of your name.

The Earliest Known Representation
of a Storm in Western Art

Like an accident or an insistence, without model or precedent,
water was rising and water would fall and flatten a picture
strung out on perspective with over-muscled jumpy horses,
men about to kneel, about to ride. The envoy whose story it was
suffered from dust, charm and the wary illumination

of bulbs that drooped from tendrils of wiring, light metered
by collection box, the cathedral's erratic pulse. I chose
a child saint who walked among victims of the plague
in a besieged city and died young. I rehearsed her name
but on that cold hard day the sky kept its distance.

I come home and the street is a river, the roof is flotsam,
chimneys are periscopes, gutters fountain, pavements lagoon.
It has rained for so long that we should have faith in it, faith
in the sea and the boat and the horses. Give me your hand,
love, look down, we are flying over our lives.

Three

Your shaved head on my thigh
evokes a third thing,
the quorum or casting vote of us

– as Aquinas struggled to fit
the perpetual quality of hair
into his logic of resurrection

so, wanting more for us,
you subtract another millimetre
from the setting of the razor's edge.

Late Sun

Dying wasps
make drunken passes at my hair.

They are drawn to glass, as air,
and cannot tell.

Up on the hill,
a garrulous crow

is testing the depth of a valley
in winter.

Jets trail
simple departure.

There are giants among us.
Tall shadows flare.